PR
You CAN COUNT ON

NATALIE GIDNEY

PROMISES YOU CAN COUNT ON

ISBN-13: 978-1-926676-42-5

Printed in Canada.

Printed by Word Alive Press
131 Cordite Road, Winnipeg, MB R3W 1S1
www.wordalivepress.ca

WORD ALIVE PRESS
Just Write!

This book is dedicated to you, the reader.
My prayer is that your life will be transformed
by the saving and loving power of my
Lord and Savior, Jesus Christ.

Acknowledgements

There are many people who have made this book possible. First, I would like to thank my incredible husband Rollie for his love and support. Thank you for your patience with me throughout this incredible journey. You are my rock. Next, to my three beautiful daughters, you have all been so understanding and patient as I have written this work and gone through the publishing process. I am so thankful that God brought each of you into our family. You are all amazing young ladies.

Thank you to Muriel Hankinson, for being a special friend and reaching out to me with the love of Christ in a time of my life when it would have been easier for you to walk away silently. I also want to thank you for taking your time to read through my manuscript and supporting me in this endeavour.

To Marion Sabine, thank you seems so insignificant for all you have done to guide me in my spiritual journey and growth. Your encouragement has been appreciated more than I can tell you. Thank you for checking my references and reading through the rough drafts, encouraging and helping me through this process.

This book would not be possible were it not for the prayers that surround it. Thank you to all of my prayer partners: Randy and Marion Sabine, Sandy and Muriel Hankinson, Terry and Sandy Stone, Rodney and Delia Mullen, Pastor Peter and Cathy Hayes, Lewis and Lorrie Sabine, and Brittany Prime. Prayer makes all things possible.

A great big thank you goes to my home church, Havelock Wesleyan. I am glad to be a part of this fellowship. You have embraced my family while praying and supporting us in so many ways. Thank you for partnering with me to make this book possible.

Thank you to all the people at Word Alive Press who have worked on this book. Your help and guidance through the publishing process has been an incredible experience. Thank you.

Most of all, I want to thank my Lord and Saviour, Jesus Christ, for transforming my life. Lord, without you, none of this would be possible. Thank you for allowing me to serve you in this way.

Introduction

Promises, promises. Everywhere you turn, someone is promising something. Turn the page of a magazine, there is a promise that you will lose ten pounds in ten days—just after Christmas. Turn on the television; ads come on one after another. One ad promises shed pounds without any effort, another promises clear skin if you use their products, still another promising a mate if you join their group of subscribers, and then a promise of knives that never need sharpening. The list goes on and on. Have you ever wondered if anyone could keep their word anymore?

There is One who means what He says, says what He means, and His promises will not be broken (Hebrews 10:23). God's promises are recorded through the Scripture everywhere. Any time we look and dig into His Word, we will unfailingly find promises that He has made and promises that He continues to keep. If we truly desire God's promises kept, we must do our part. There are things that He desires and commands of us.

The question is not about whether He wants to, or if He is able. The question is, "Are you willing? Are you willing to submit your life to something much greater than yourself?" If you have answered yes, then you will not be sorry.

We serve a God who loves us much more than we could ever imagine. God's love is ever present and a source of comfort in times of trouble and in times of rejoicing. I don't recommend that you wait until you are down-and-out to seek God. But even if you do, it is never too late. God is our Heavenly Father, and His love knows no end.

If you are married, think about how much you love your spouse. If you have children, think about how much you love them. If you are a grandparent, think about your love for your grandchildren. God's love is much bigger than all of these pulled together. We cannot begin to fathom the love God has for each one of us. The Bible tells us, "*for God is love*" (1 John 4:8).

We must believe that He is telling us the truth. All that matters is the faith we have in Him. He can do the unimaginable and He *wants to*. God's love is so deep and wide for us. He wants what is best for us and He will encourage us to come to Him in our hardships. Don't we want our children, family, and friends to come to us with their problems rather than going to someone else? How much more do you think our Heavenly Father wants us to come to Him with our needs, desires, and wants?

God wants to envelop us in love. He wants us to know that we can come to Him always. God is there no matter what. It is up to us to keep that line of communication open. When we do, we will find that He is there without exception. That is the purpose of this book, to explore some of the promises held within the most important book you will ever read. A book that never goes out of style. A book that is treasured throughout the ages as a manual for an incredible life. The Bible.

If you are hungry for promises you can always count on, read on. I recommend that you keep your Bible handy and check the references. I pray that the God of the ages will speak directly to your heart, revealing His love and the promises He has in store for you. Get ready for promises you can count on!

Table of Contents

CHAPTER ONE

THE BEGINNING OF THE PROMISE

Before I knew Jesus on a personal level, I felt that my life was worth nothing. I was ready to give it all up and pack it in. At that point in time, I had three small children and a husband who depended on me day to day, but I still had this deep, dark feeling of worthlessness. In that pit of depression and despair, I truly believed that my family and this world that we live in would be so much better without me in it.

One night after my husband went to work, I called a friend just to chat (at least, that was my intention). Once we got talking I told her that I needed her to come and see me. It was as if I had another person speaking for me. As the words were coming out of my mouth, my head was screaming and every fibre of my being was in a state of sheer and utter panic. Shock flooded my whole being; body, mind, and spirit. What would I do when she arrived? Could I lie and tell her I was fine?

That day, something much bigger than me was in control and I was afraid of it, yet there was a certain release and peace in letting go. I had told someone I was in trouble. I revealed a need I had to another person. I really couldn't believe it, because for so many years I hid my hurts and put on a mask of happiness.

Thank God she came right away. By the time she got there I had convinced my logical self that I would tell her I just needed a friend to have a coffee with. But for some reason that night, my mouth did not operate on logic. Again I felt helpless, as if someone else had taken over and knew my most private and personal thoughts and feelings. Something or someone bigger was at work in me.

I poured out all that I was feeling, history from my past that had kept me in bondage, and she just looked at me. Her mouth dropped open, but no words came out. Her eyes softened. I felt almost naked, as if someone was seeing the real, whole me for the first time. We had known each other for close to sixteen years at that point and she didn't know the real me, only what I was willing for her and everyone else to see. She had no idea what was going on in the innermost parts of my mind and soul. No one did.

We had lived in close proximity for a year when we were both at college, yet I masked the hurts so well that no one knew anything of my heartaches and pain. I was so angry. Angry at the world. Angry at being abandoned by my dad. Angry at my mum. Angry at everyone and everything.

I felt so alone, even with my children and husband around me all the time. I could be completely surrounded by people who loved me and cared about me, but I still felt alone, as if I was drowning and no one cared.

She remained quiet for a time while I tried to pull myself together. I remember wiping tears away from my bloodshot eyes. I couldn't help but think, *She must think I am totally crazy. Right out to lunch. What have I done? She must be waiting for a way to get out of this nuthouse I call home.* But that was not at all what she shared with me; even if she did think it.

I don't remember the exact words she used, but she looked me squarely in the eyes and told me that I needed to read the Bible. Just like that! She boldly looked me in the face and told me that it was God I needed. I'm not sure if she sent up an emergency prayer at that time in the quiet of her heart or not, but she let me have it. She knew just what I needed. And she didn't stop there. She also invited me to church. She hit me with reality.

A great heaping dose of reality. Reality of a Creator who loves me. Reality of a God who sent His only Son to die on a cross for me. Reality that God knew and understood exactly what I was going through. Reality that whatever I was going through, I was not alone.

I want to make something exceedingly clear. God knows your pain, He knows your hurt, He knows all there is to know about you. Psalm 139:13 says, "*For you created my inmost being; you knit me together in my mother's womb*" (NIV). He put us together one stitch at a time. He knows how many hairs are on your head. God has the hairs on your head not only counted, but numbered (Matthew 10:30). God loves you with an immeasurable love. That is why He sent His one and only Son, Jesus Christ, to die on that cross for *you*.

That evening I spent bearing my heart was the springboard into my spiritual formation and understanding of who God the Creator, Jesus His Son, and the Holy Spirit are. I understand that God was very much at work that night and He's had me ever since. There is so much I don't know yet, but the Spirit reveals truths as we are ready for them (John 16:13). I pray the truths that have been revealed to me that I am sharing in this book will challenge you to dig deeper, pray more, and search for answers about who God is and how much He loves you. I challenge you to make your relationship with Him so personal that it hurts to be away from Him.

Before she left that night, my friend asked me if I had a Bible. I answered yes. She explained that I needed to read my Bible and suggested that I start with the book of John. She knew that I was a reader and also recommended the *Left Behind* series by Tim LaHaye and Jerry Jenkins. She dropped them off to me a couple at a time until I had read them all. In just a few months, I devoured them. Every minute I had to sit, I would read.

During that time of struggle, all I wanted was peace. Peace had never been within my grasp. I had always felt that something was missing. As I read through the book of John, I read Jesus' promise of peace. In John 16:33 Jesus says, "*These things I have spoken to you, that in Me you may have peace. In the world you will have tribulation; but be of good cheer, I have overcome the world.*" Jesus' words. "In Me you may have peace." What a promise! Jesus promises to give us peace.

Peace is a strange thing. When we have it, we don't really notice it and tend to take it for granted. When we don't, we are aching in our heart for something, but most often cannot put into words what it is. This passage explains to us that our peace is in Him, Jesus. He wants to bless us with a free gift that can change lives and turn around even the most unlikely soul. The peace of Christ is right in front of you. All there is to do is make the decision and reach out for it, grab it, and claim it for your own.

Remember that Jesus didn't promise smooth sailing in life. He did say that there would be trials, but that our peace is in Him. We must learn more and more about who He is to find that peace we seek. In my search to find peace, I have found many more promises (and I'm continuing to find more) that He has made to each of us. God is so amazing.

A man in my Sunday school class once said, "We will probably never be able to know how God thinks. Our small minds are not equipped to even begin to understand in the way that He does." It is so true. In the book of Isaiah, God reveals this truth to us. "'*For My thoughts are not your thoughts, nor are your ways My ways,' says the Lord. 'For as the heavens are higher than the earth, so are My ways higher than your ways, and My thoughts than your thoughts*'" (Isaiah 55:8-9).

One thing I do know. His love is an unconditional, all-consuming love. How great it is to know that we can be loved in such a way. I pray that as you read this book you will seek out God's promises for you. Claim them and watch and see what He can do. I'm sure you will be utterly amazed by what He is able to do with your life if you fully surrender to His will and work in His strength.

CHAPTER TWO

THE PROMISE OF SALVATION

God desires to be our Heavenly Father. He longs to have a personal, Father-child relationship with each person He has created. To become one of His children, one must be saved. What does that mean and how can we get there? Salvation means deliverance. We all need deliverance from the sinful state we were born into. It is a choice made in the heart between each one of us and God Himself. How do we make that choice?

First of all, we need to genuinely admit the fact that we are all sinners and we cannot save ourselves, but that we need an intercessor. That intercessor is Jesus Christ. The Bible teaches us that no amount of good works or well thought out and executed intentions can bring us life in Heaven with God. Neither money nor position, or even power, can buy a place in Heaven. Jesus tells us in John 14:6, "*I am the way, the truth, and the life. No one comes to the Father except through Me.*" This is very clear. Jesus wants us to know that there is a way to spend eternity in Heaven. It is through Jesus and Jesus alone.

When God created man, He made him in His own image and likeness (Genesis 1:27). Let's try to envision what God had in mind for mankind as He was creating Adam and Eve. Just picture them in a perfect setting, the most beautiful garden full of all the most beautiful things you can imagine.

You are standing in the middle of the most lush, amazing place you have ever seen or imagined. As your eyes long to take it all in, they take a long pause on the river flowing through the garden. The river sparkles as if dancing and laughing in the sunlight. Trees bend their branches at the water's edge, longing to touch the crisp, clear water. Rose bushes bloom, great gorgeous flowers with the most vibrant colors and amazing smells. Herbs sway to and fro in the gentle breezes. Flowing, cascading branches of apple, plum, and peach trees are heavy laden with full, succulent fruit. Your nose delights at the wonderful smells floating on the gentle breeze.

You look down for a moment and notice rich, green, velvety-soft grass carpeting your steps as you walk with your Creator in the loveliest place ever created. You look up to see animals and birds with the richest colors and grandest spots and stripes you could ever imagine. Your heart is overflowing with love. You are full of peace in His presence. This is the kind of world that God wanted His people to live in. He wanted us to marvel at His handiwork, bask in the glory that is His alone. When He completed all of these things, they were very good (Genesis 1:31).

Adam and Eve had a wonderful existence. No worries, no stress, no problems of any kind. They were never annoyed by mosquitoes or black flies biting them. They never had to think about being attacked by a wild animal in the woods. Their lives were perfect. They had the privilege to experience the perfect temperature, the perfect sunrise and the perfect sunset each and every day. They were met in the garden by their Creator and communed with Him face to face (Genesis 3:8). What an amazing existence.

Then something happened. Suddenly you are transported back to reality. You are in a sin-filled world. Picture the poorest place on earth you can think of. Imagine the stench of the water you must bathe in, water that is also used as a public toilet. Consider giving your child a drink that will probably kill her from that same hole you bathed in and earlier used as a toilet. But you have no choice. This is where you live. This is what sin has done.

But, you may say, I live in a beautiful home on a beautiful street with a wonderful family. I have good friends and we give to the poor. We give our tithes to the church every Sunday. I teach Sunday school, work on the Missions Committee, and even give my time for the Children's Mid-Week Program. These are all wonderful things.

On the other hand, look into your heart. Maybe with some honesty you will see jealousy and envy. You may flip back a corner of your heart and find gossiping. You may look in a crevice and find greed or anger and rage.

Off in another place, unforgiveness seethes within. There may be a whole host of sinful behaviours that you need to allow God to deal with. All of these are directly related to that first bit of disobedience in the Garden of Eden with Adam and Eve.

One day, as Eve was enjoying herself; the serpent showed himself and began a conversation with her. He insinuated that God, the God she knew and loved, was trying to hide something from her. He coaxed her to eat of the one tree that God had forbidden her to eat from. He made his case so convincingly that she fell into the trap of entertaining his lies and listening to what he had to say. She believed him and ate of the tree, and then gave some to her husband to eat. That incident was an act of direct disobedience to God (for a full account, read Genesis 3).

Satan is a liar (John 8:44). When he brings something up, we may recognize it as a lie and then try to defend ourselves. In opening a line of communication with the enemy, we take a step away from God. Whether we believe Satan's lies or not, entering into a conversation with him can lead us down a path we will regret. If Eve had left the presence of Satan and not begun the conversation with him, she may not have fallen into his trap of lies and deceit, a trap that led to the beginning of sin and disobedience.

The sin that was committed that day separated all humans from God. God is perfect and He hates sin. Sin must be forgiven for us to live life in the presence of God. Because of that, we must recognize that we are all sinners and the penalty for sin is death (Romans 6:23).

God gave Adam and Eve free will, just as He gives to all of us. Sometimes it allows us to make some horrendous mistakes. The enemy, Satan, is very real and he wants us to be miserable. The worst thing we can do is to even acknowledge his lies and engage in conversation with him. He is a deceiver and wants to do you harm (1 Peter 5:8). He doesn't want you to walk in God's way and, just as he deceived Eve, he will try anything to deceive you.

Your only defence is faith in God and prayer. Pray for God to open your heart and eyes and allow Him to show you His truth and His way. If Eve had relied on God and asked for His direction in her decision, the world as we know it would be a totally different place.

Our built-in desire is to "fit in," but many times we don't know where that is. Some may feel that social clubs and money, or power and prestige can fill that hole, but they are running away from the truth that will fill that spot. It's like trying to put a square peg in a round hole. However hard you try, you will never accomplish a complete or perfect fit. It is the same way in our hearts and souls.

There is a place where nothing fits but Jesus. You can try to fill that hole with drugs, sex, alcohol, money, power, or a whole range of other things, but nothing will fit. That is because when God created us, He created us to love Him. There is only one thing that will fit in that hole. What fits is Jesus.

God knew that we could not follow the laws as set out in the Old Testament and so He had a plan for a new covenant. The truth of the new covenant was revealed to

Jeremiah in the Old Testament. When God spoke to Jeremiah, these were the words He spoke. "*Behold, the days are coming, says the Lord, when I will make a new covenant with the house of Israel and with the house of Judah—not according to the covenant that I made with their fathers in the day that I took them by the hand to lead them out of the land of Egypt, My covenant which they broke, though I was a husband to them, says the Lord. But this is the covenant that I will make with the house of Israel after those days, says the Lord: I will put My law in their minds, and write it on their hearts; and I will be their God, and they shall be My people. No more shall every man teach his neighbour, and every man his brother, saying, 'Know the Lord,' for they shall know Me, from the least of them to the greatest of them, says the Lord. For I will forgive their iniquity, and their sin I will remember no more*" (Jeremiah 31:31-34).

With the New Covenant came the promise of a Saviour, Jesus Christ. God would send His one and only Son to save us. Jesus came into the world as a King, not looking for servants, but to serve. He loved us so much that He wanted to make a way that all mankind could be acceptable before God the Father. He was born of the Virgin Mary (Matthew 1:20-21). Jesus grew to teach and train disciples and then left us with the Great Commission to make disciples of all the nations (Matthew 28:19-20).

Jesus bridged a chasm between humankind and God that we could not manoeuvre without His help. The cross created a bridge so that we could all now be acceptable before God (John 3:16). In the Old Testament, the sacrifices needed to be perfect, without blemish, sacrificed before the High Priest. Sacrifices were made to atone for the sins of the Israelites. Just as they needed to make sacrifices and ask for forgiveness, so must we.

However, when we ask for forgiveness, we do not need to sacrifice an animal. We have a Great High Priest to come before. This promise is recorded in the book of Hebrews. "*For we do not have a High Priest who cannot sympathize with our weaknesses, but was in all points tempted as we are, yet without sin. Let us therefore come boldly to the throne of grace, that we may obtain mercy and find grace to help in times of need*" (Hebrews 4:15-16).

Jesus was the perfect sacrifice for all humankind all those years ago. "*For He made Him who knew no sin to be sin for us, that we might become the righteousness of God in Him*" (2 Corinthians 5:21). Jesus did not ever commit a sin against anyone on earth or His Father in Heaven, therefore He was the perfect sacrifice. God's wrath needed to be satisfied, and for that reason we can claim the work done by Jesus on the cross. He took our sins upon Himself. That is how much God loves each of us. Romans 5:8-9 explains it perfectly. "*But God demonstrates His own love toward us, in that while we were still sinners, Christ died for us. Much more then, having now been justified by His blood, we shall be saved from wrath through Him.*"

Some of Jesus' final words as He died a painful and humiliating death were, "It is finished." (John 19:30) He finished the task that His Father had given Him. He created a way for God's people to have a personal relationship with Him once again. Through Jesus' shed blood on the cross, we all can stand before God, "*being justified freely by His grace through the redemption that is in Christ Jesus"* (Romans 3:24). Jesus Christ purchased our freedom. He paid the price for sinners now and forevermore.

We must believe and have faith in the power of God who sent His one and only Son to live a sinless life (Luke 1:35). Isaiah prophesied that He would suffer a painful and horrible death (Isaiah 52:13-14). Then Jesus rose from death to be seated at the right hand of the Father to be an intercessor for "*the whosoever will*" (Romans 8:34).

One mistake I made after giving my life to Christ was thinking that all things would be so easy. I had a rose-colored glasses outlook. I believed that my faith in Him would protect me from hurt and heartache. Boy, was I wrong. I was so frustrated when things began to get tough and pile on top of me.

My world was shaking and I went to a Christian woman I had grown to love and respect (and continue to). I poured my heart and soul out to her. By the time I finished, I was a mess of tears, begging for her help and wisdom in this situation. I felt like I had been misled. I had thought that the Christian life would be one of ease and comfort. What an error in judgment!

She explained John 16:33. Jesus was teaching His disciples. "*These things I have spoken to you, that in Me you may have peace. In this world you will have tribulation; but be of good cheer, I have overcome the world*" (emphasis mine). Jesus tells us, just as He told His disciples, that we will have times of trials and tribulation, but that He will give us His peace. Also, in studying Scripture, we find that many Christians suffered. Paul, the first missionary in the Bible, was well-acquainted with suffering. 2 Corinthians 11:24-28 will give you a bit of insight into the suffering Paul encountered.

There is nowhere in Scripture that says life will be easy and breezy if you accept the Lord Jesus Christ into your life. I've looked. I've searched. I've asked people who are pastors and teachers, some for forty years or more. It is not there. Jesus tells us that we will have tribulation. He never said it would be easy, but He did say, "*I will never leave you nor forsake you*" (Hebrews 13:5).

Another reassurance of His presence comes from John 14:27. "*Peace I leave with you, My peace I give to you; not as the world gives do I give to you. Let not your heart be troubled, neither let it be afraid.*" He also promises that He has overcome the world. We can rest in the promise that He is in control. If we look to God, we will never go wrong.

Life with Christ may not be easy, but the life you will gain—peace, love, forgiveness, eternal life and so many other blessings—will outweigh all the rest. You will have troubles, but now you have God to lean on. You have an open line of communication with the one and only Almighty God who is available 24/7, and that is worth any price you must pay.

Your faith in the Lord Jesus Christ is paramount to your salvation. Without it, there is no eternal life in heaven. A simple way to pray and receive salvation is to first admit that you are a sinner, for all fall short of the glory of God (Romans 3:23), realizing that the penalty for being a sinner is death (Romans 6:23). Next, you must believe that Jesus Christ died for your sins (Romans 5:8). Lastly, you need to commit your life to Him.

Confess that He is Lord of your life. Romans 10:8-10 states, "*But what does it say? 'The word is near you, in your mouth and in your heart' (that is, the word of faith which we preach): that if you confess with your mouth the Lord Jesus and believe in your heart that God has raised Him from the dead, you will be saved. For with the heart one believes unto righteousness, and with the mouth confession is made unto salvation.*"

Therefore, it must be a sincere heart, mind, and spirit choice. You need to make this decision totally for yourself. Salvation is dependant upon each person accepting Christ. No one can do it for you. You cannot do it for anyone else. It is as individual as your fingerprint. If you do not know how to word your prayer and would like to accept Jesus Christ as your personal Saviour, turn to the appendix for a prayer to guide you.

Salvation is a promise from God that you can count on. Trust Him to lead you in all that you do and you will be filled with His love and peace that no money can buy. Remember, Jesus said, "*I am the way, the truth, and the life. No one comes to the Father except through me*" (John 14:6, emphasis mine).

CHAPTER THREE

THE PROMISE OF WISDOM AND GUIDANCE

When Jesus lived on this earth about two thousand years ago, He taught and trained His disciples to love, heal, and pray (just to name a few). He walked with them and talked with them. He taught by example. Think about how great it would have been to walk those miles in the presence of Jesus, sitting at His feet, learning from the Master. Wow!

There is a story in the book of John (the sixth chapter) that describes a time when Jesus' disciples were in His amazing presence. Let me give you an overview. Imagine being on that hillside all those years ago. Jesus was going up on the mountain to rest with His disciples. When He looked up, He noticed a crowd of people gathering around Him. He took note that it was coming on mealtime and inquired of Philip where they should buy bread to feed these people. (Remember that Jesus knew what He would do and therefore was testing Philip.) Philip must have been shocked. He couldn't possibly see how so many people could be fed without money.

Andrew, going into the crowd, found a young boy with five barley loaves and two small fish. He took them to Jesus. Jesus then asked the disciples to get the people to sit. It is recorded that about five thousand were there that day. "*And Jesus took the loaves, and when He had given thanks He distributed them to the disciples, and the disciples to those sitting down; and likewise of the fish, as much as they wanted. So when they were filled, He said to His disciples, 'Gather up the fragments that remain, so that nothing is lost*'" (John 6:11-12). Then the disciples gathered the leftover food from among the crowd, and brought it to Him. After all the people had eaten, there were still twelve full baskets (for a full account, read John 6:1-15).

Twelve full baskets. After five thousand people had eaten from five loaves and two fish, there was still enough food to fill twelve baskets. Andrew had brought this boy and his food before Jesus Christ. There was scarcely enough there to fill two baskets in the beginning, yet Scripture records that Jesus gave thanks to His Father in Heaven and the baskets were filled repeatedly until all of the five thousand were fed that day. However, the story does not end there. In the end, everything was gathered up and there were twelve full baskets left over.

That is the power of the God we serve. Really stop and think about how great it would have been to be in Jesus' presence all those years ago feeding five thousand people with five loaves and two fishes. Can you imagine being there? Picture yourself walking on that mountainside, feet and tunic dusty and dirty. Your legs exhausted from all the walking. Your stomach growling and burning with pangs of hunger. As you look down the mountainside, it is almost alive with movement. There are people hiking right behind you, anxious to hear another word from the Master.

Unfortunately, we cannot go back in time to see this miracle being performed, but we do have access to something even more special. When Jesus was preparing to leave this earth, He told His followers, "*And I will pray the Father, and He will give you another Helper, that He may abide with you forever—the Spirit of truth, whom the world cannot receive, because it neither sees Him nor knows Him; but you know Him, for He dwells with you and will be in you*" (John 14:16-18). Jesus promised a Helper, the Holy Spirit.

When Jesus left this earth, He did not leave us alone to fend for ourselves. He did not want us to fumble along in life, wandering and lost, hopeless and fearful. He wanted to bless us with power from on high. So he sent the Holy Spirit. In many ways, I think we are every bit as fortunate, and maybe even more so in some ways, than the people who walked with Jesus. Though in Jesus' day people were able to touch and see Him perform miracles, they did not have the power of the Holy Spirit within themselves. That didn't happen until Jesus left this earth.

We have access to power that is unimaginable if we claim it and accept it. When we claim Jesus Christ as our personal Saviour, we can receive the incredible gift of the Holy Spirit that dwells within us to guide our lives. Acts 2:38-39 says, "*Then Peter said to them, 'Repent, and let every one of you be baptized in the name of Jesus Christ for the remission of sins; and you shall receive the gift of the Holy Spirit. For the promise is to you and to your children, and all who are afar off, <u>as many as the Lord our God will call</u>*" (emphasis mine). It is a promise that Jesus made to each and every one of us. We no longer have to wonder or walk around not knowing; we have the ability to pray for the Spirit to lead us in all things we do.

One wonderful yet difficult thing about the Spirit is the conviction He doles out. He may convict you of sin in the moment you commit it. If you are obedient and truly ask forgiveness, God's grace covers that sin. 1 John 1:9 states, "*If we confess our sins, He is faithful and just to forgive us our sins and to cleanse us from all unrighteousness.*" Not only does He shower us with forgiveness, but He also gives us the ability to avoid future encounters with that sin. However, if you are convicted and do not repent, you will begin to feel a distance from the Spirit and it becomes harder to hear His voice.

The Spirit is given to us to guide and direct us (John 16:13). It is our responsibility to obey and be "tuned in" to the truth. It is very difficult to tune a radio station if you do not know the frequency. You may know the name, but if you don't know the number on the dial, you will not hear that station.

The same holds true for the Holy Spirit. We must learn to hear the Spirit and His promptings, and then act on them. Having the words of the Scriptures hidden in our hearts (Psalm 119:11), helps us to know God on a more intimate level and hear more clearly (John 14:21).

To know the voice of the Spirit, we must first understand that the Holy Spirit is, in fact, God. The Spirit will never prompt us to do anything contrary to the Word of God. Studying Scripture and knowing the truth will help you to discern the Spirit's promptings. If you are unsure, search the Scripture for the truth. Allow God to guide your life in all you do.

The Holy Spirit gives us a boldness (Acts 4:31) to deliver God's message to others, whether as a preacher preaching a sermon, a teacher teaching God's Word, a member of the congregation giving a testimony, or as a neighbour sharing the news of Jesus Christ's redemptive power. Without the Spirit, no one would be able to do these things. We must give the Spirit room to do His work, trust in what He is asking us to do, and then step out in faith and do it.

How do you know that you are working in the power of the Spirit? *"But the fruit of the Spirit is love, joy, peace, patience, kindness, goodness, faithfulness, gentleness and self control. Against such things there is no law"* (Galatians 5:22-23, NIV). If we live in accordance with these truths, we will not grieve the Spirit. However, if we live contrary to these things, we will live further and further away from the will of God for our lives (Galatians 5:19-21).

Think about it. God doesn't tempt us to sin. This we must remember. It is easy to blame God for our bad days, our misunderstandings, and our failings, but it is time we direct ourselves in truth. "*Jesus said to him, 'I am the way, the truth, and the life. No one comes to the Father except through Me*'" (John 14:6, emphasis mine).

Satan is the father of lies, the master deceiver (John 8:44). When guilt and condemnation rule our lives, the Spirit is no longer in control. We have gotten off track somewhere along the road and moved further and further away from the Lord. But it is not too late. You can get back on the straight and narrow path of righteousness. Ask for forgiveness and pray for the Holy Spirit to take control of your life. Just wait and see what He can do when you ask.

CHAPTER FOUR

THE PROMISE OF GOD'S LOVE

John 3:16 says, "*For God so loved the world that He gave His only begotten Son, that whoever believes in Him should not perish but have everlasting life.*" Whoever! That means everlasting life is a promise available to anyone who believes. There are no strings attached and no conditions apply. There aren't any late fees or down-payments required.

God's love is a free gift to anyone who will believe in the glorious gift of Jesus' death on the cross and the resurrection of the body. We know that Jesus is alive today and He is coming back someday (Acts 1:9-11, Revelation 1:8). Why did Jesus do all these things? His love for us is so great. He does not want us to live life apart from Him.

Do you have children? If not, do you have a niece or a nephew? Or think of a friend's child whom you absolutely adore. Now think of someone asking you to allow that child to die a horrible and painful death to save another. Would you do it? Would you allow that precious child to be tortured and beaten down, suffer a painful and humiliating death to take the place of any other person on this earth?

If you are like me, the answer would be a loud and resounding NO! But this has happened. God sent His Son, Jesus Christ, to this earth to be a man who would willingly suffer and die for each and every person who believes in Him.

Stop and think about that for a few minutes. Really meditate on that truth. You don't have to pay Him, you needn't bribe Him. You don't have to beg or plead with Him. All that is required is for each person to believe. *Believe*. That is all. But wait a minute. What does it really mean to believe?

According to the Student Bible Dictionary, the word believe means "to have confidence in, have faith in, make a commitment to."[1] This is much more than words coming out of the mouth. We cannot just say the words "I believe." When we say "I believe in Christ and the work that was done on the cross," we must have faith and confidence without wavering or doubt. When someone asks you if you believe in Christ and what He has done for you, your answer should scream out "Yes!" throughout your heart and soul. The word yes should not just be on your lips. You should feel it in your innermost being, convinced who Christ truly is.

The way you live your life should reflect the love of Jesus Christ in all ways. People you meet should see

---

[1] *The Student Bible Dictionary*. Barbour Publishing, Inc., Uhrichsville, Ohio. Used by permission.

God's love in your eyes (compassion and empathy), in your hands (the things you do), and in your heart (the compassion and love you show for others). While Jesus was on this earth, He loved everyone. He didn't have favourites.

Many times, we ask people, "How are you today?" Our compassion and empathy truly shine through when we take the time to listen and connect with them. People in the world (and in the church) today are hurting. We can train ourselves to show the love of Christ to total strangers by truly listening and having an open heart, receiving their answer, and showing them we care. We all want someone to listen to us. We all desire for someone to take the time to care about our hurts. Extending that same concern to a total stranger demonstrates the love God shares with us.

Believing is stepping out in faith where it is totally uncomfortable. Believing is knowing that God is real and that He will carry you when you fall. Believing is knowing His Son is real and that they both love you completely. Yes, you! We all need to acknowledge the truth way down deep inside that Jesus is the only way to eternal life. He's it. There is no other way. There is no alternate route—no detours, no shortcuts. It's all Jesus and nothing else. *"Jesus said to him, 'I am the way, the truth, and the life. No one comes to the Father except through Me'"* (John 14:6).

God's love for us is a love that cannot be measured. His love is as far as the east is from the west. The north and south poles are on every globe, marked so all know where they are, but the east and west truly go on forever. Wherever you are in the world, there is always another place to the east and more places to the west. It is truly amazing to think about. God's love has no limit, no boundaries. That is how big His love is for us.

His love sent His Son to the cross to die so that we could be with Him. God's love for humankind poured all the sins of the world onto Jesus and was then nailed on the cross with Him. The sacrifice that was made satisfied the wrath of God so that we could stand cleansed, free from sin, brothers and sisters with Christ. His love bridged a gap that was so wide very few could get to Him, but now "*whoever believes in Him should not perish but have everlasting life*" (John 3:16).

That is how much each one of us is cherished. The act of obedience that took Him to the cross allows every one of us a way to eternal life. Whatever the sin, whatever the mistake, whatever you have done or not done—God is willing to forgive. All that is required is a humbling of the mind and soul, acknowledging your sinful state and asking His forgiveness. With faith in your heart and a willingness to accept His divine forgiveness, He will forgive every sin.

God's love is big enough that not only does He forgive, but Micah 7:19 says, "*You will again have compassion on us; you will tread our sins underfoot and hurl all our iniquities into the depths of the sea*" (NIV). He has promised to completely forgive our sins. He will never throw our mistakes back in our faces. That is true love.

Do you believe Him when He says He loves you? Do you allow Him to lead your life? If not, you may want to begin to develop a connection with Jesus Christ that will secure your faith and make it unshakeable. How do you do this?

We discussed salvation in the first step (Chapter 2). We've also talked about reading and studying the Bible. Just looking at the Bible can make reading it seem like an impossible task. It is a huge book. Where to start? I suggest starting at the book of John in the New Testament. John is where I was directed when I first began.

It is amazing to read the accounts of the miracles performed by Jesus and what He went through for us. Develop a habit of reading your Bible daily, expecting to meet with the Lord. You can read whole chapters, or you may want to meditate on a verse that speaks to you in one way or another.

Another step that I can never stress enough is prayer. Prayer is crucial to your relationship with the Lord. Developing a prayer life that is consistent will help you to experience God's love. Each time you set aside time to pray and go into His presence, you will be changed. His love will begin to fill you, bit by bit, if you truly seek Him. Your time spent with the Lord will increase your faith tremendously. However, learn to listen as well as talk. Pour your heart out to Him, but learn to sit in silence to hear His voice. God speaks with "*a still small voice*" (1 Kings 19:12).

When Elijah wanted to hear from God, he went to Mount Sinai. He was feeling overwhelmed and discouraged after two significant spiritual victories. First, he defeated the prophets of Baal at Mount Carmel (1 Kings

18:20-40), then God answered his prayer for rainfall (1 Kings 18:41-45).

Once Jezebel found out Elijah killed all the prophets of Baal, she fiercely threatened him and fear overtook him to the point of fleeing. Not only did he flee, but he prayed for God to take his life. Fear made him forget God's promises. However, God's love for Elijah brought him back to his senses. You can read this account in 1 Kings 19.

God doesn't give up on us. He doesn't throw His hands up in the air and say, "Whatever!" or "Forget it!" He gently nudges us and lovingly holds us. If we are willing and open, He will remind us of who He is. Again, we must learn to recognize and listen to His voice. Sometimes God speaks to our hearts, and sometimes He speaks through other Christians in our lives. He may even speak to us through our circumstances. One thing is for sure: He does speak.

When Moses asked to see God's glory, God took him up the mountain and placed him in a crevice. As He passed by Moses, God covered Moses' eyes until He had passed by. Then all Moses could see was His glory from behind. From behind. Moses saw the glory of God, not head on, but after He had passed by. Even then his face shone in such a way that he needed to wear a veil so that the Israelites could look on him (Exodus 33:18-23).

We know God by what *He* does. We cannot understand who He is except through Jesus Christ. God's love for us is truly amazing. To remember God's promises is to "engrave" them on your heart. Memorize Scripture. We are quick to lead our children to memorize Scripture, yet as adults we tend to think of it as unimportant. It is extremely important. In times of trouble or distress, you may not have your Bible or the time to open it. If you have placed those verses on your heart, you can call on them 24/7, remembering and truly knowing the love of God.

I have heard it said that twenty-one days develops a habit. Once you begin spending time with the Lord on a regular basis, you will really miss it if you do not make it a priority. Try it for twenty-one days and see if it makes a difference in your life. There is nothing to lose and everything to gain.

Remember, God loves you. His love is unshakeable because of the work Jesus did on the cross at Calvary all those years ago. There is nothing you can do to earn His love except ask Jesus into your heart and believe in what He has done for *you*. Yes, He did it for you, me, and everyone on the face of this earth who will call upon His name. Nothing is too horrible to be forgiven. Step out in faith, believe, and ask. Just watch what God can do with a willing heart focused on Him. He will absolutely and utterly astound you. Prepare to be amazed.

CHAPTER FIVE

The Promise of Grace

As a little girl, I marvelled at the sight of a ballet dancer. The motion, the movement, the flow. Such charm and grace. I, however, was not quite so graceful. I was more likely to trip over my own two feet than do a pirouette. That didn't stop me from watching with wonder and amazement at the beauty of those dancers.

It is not the grace of a dancer that I want to talk about in this chapter, though. It is the favour of God, so full of love that His heart overflows with grace for each one of His children. I have been humbled many times when I've seen His grace in action.

Every night before I go to bed, I look in on my three beautiful daughters. They are so precious and look so sweet; faces so innocent and peaceful. By God's grace, I have the privilege to hold these children closely for a time. There was a time I thought I would never have children. I was told that because of polycystic ovarian syndrome, I would probably not be able to conceive naturally, and maybe never at all. I was heartbroken.

My husband and I decided not to even try for five years, because we wanted to do some traveling before settling into a family routine. Thinking it was going to take a long time to conceive, we decided to start trying to get pregnant going into our fourth year of marriage. Within three months, I was pregnant. What joy! What wonderful grace God bestowed on us, and after such a short time. After our first was born, we decided to have another as soon as we could and I got pregnant again. Before our oldest was four, I had given birth to three beautiful daughters.

Looking back, I now know that God has always loved me so much, even when I felt He didn't even know I existed. His grace is so far reaching. He can pull you out of the slime and muck, wipe the tears, clean you up, give you new clothes, and set your feet on steady ground. He did it for me and He will do it for you. He has a plan for every person He puts on this earth. We know this is true because He spoke these words to Jeremiah: "*'For I know the plans I have for you,' declares the Lord, 'plans to prosper you and not harm you, plans to give you hope and a future*" (Jeremiah 29:11 NIV). His grace is what allows us to be so very blessed by a personal relationship with Him if we will choose it. The grace He offers is undeserved favour. In other words, it can never be earned.

In Ephesians 2:8-9, Paul explains what grace is. "*For by grace you have been saved through faith, and that not of your-*

selves; it is the gift of God, not of works, lest anyone should boast." There is not one person who has enough money, talent, or position to earn God's grace. You cannot buy it, you cannot earn it, you cannot work hard enough to get it. It is through faith that we are granted grace. Faith is the key that unlocks the door to the grace of God.

We must have faith to know that God will do what He promises. How do we get there? To begin with, we can read His Word. The Bible is His way of reaching us. Romans 10:17 puts it clearly: "*So then faith comes by hearing, and hearing by the word of God.*" I've heard it said that the word Bible stands for "Basic Instructions Before Leaving Earth." What an awesome God we have. Not only does He go with us wherever we go, but He has given us a book to lead and guide our lives. He has given us everything we need. It is an instruction manual for living. Reading His written Word daily will guide our spiritual growth and knowledge in His ways. The more we read, the more of an in-focus picture of God we will have.

Another thing to do is meditate on the Scriptures that God reveals to your heart as significant. Memorizing and knowing Scripture by heart is a great way to see God's grace in action. One of my favourite verses, when I'm feeling fearful, is Psalm 27:1. "*The Lord is my light and my salvation; whom shall I fear? The Lord is the strength of my life; of whom shall I be afraid?*" Knowing that I have the ability to call on that verse any time I am in need, any place I may be, is wonderfully comforting. Memorizing Scripture is like tattooing God's Word on your heart. Once it is there, no one can take it away.

He wants us to grow in faith and knowledge of who He is. Romans 4:16 states that Abraham's faith was enough. How hard would it be to believe that you and your wife would have a child in your old age, years after menopause? It would be unfathomable, unreasonable, and absolutely ridiculous. It seemed so crazy, Abraham laughed when God told him (Genesis 17:17). Abraham, like everyone else, made some mistakes, but God told him that He would have a son with Sarah and He fulfilled that promise (see Genesis 21:2 for the fulfillment of the promise).

In Genesis 22, God tested Abraham. When God asked Abraham to sacrifice his son on a mountain, Abraham did not question Him; he took Isaac and had faith. As they were preparing to make the sacrifice, Isaac inquired about the lamb for the offering. Abraham replied, "*My son, God will provide for Himself the lamb for a burnt offering*" (Genesis 22:8). By that time Abraham knew enough about God's grace to take Him at His word. That is also true for us. We need to develop our faith in the one true God and His promise of grace.

How will we ever truly know God? By spending time with Him, we learn who He is. Our responsibility in the relationship is to spend time with Him—in His Word, in silence, and in prayer. Like any relationship, our relationship with the Lord needs to be nurtured. Would you expect your close friends to be there for you if you were never there for them? Not really. The same holds true for our relationship with Jesus, we must take time to be in His presence, pray, and listen closely.

God promises at the end of Hebrews 13:5, "*I will never leave you nor forsake you.*" This is an excellent piece of Scripture to memorize. After we have it memorized, we should strive to live like we really believe it. He will always be close, but whether we can fathom His presence depends on our faith and trust in Him.

That does not necessarily mean that nothing bad will ever happen to you again, but it does mean that whatever you encounter, Jesus will be right there beside you. His grace will see you through anything you must go through, good, bad, or in between. His grace is a free gift from a heart that is bursting forth, full of love for each one of us. That is why God laid out the path for Jesus to follow to the cross, to be the perfect sacrifice.

God, who loves us so very much, saw the significance of the life of each person on this earth. "*For God so loved the world that He gave His only begotten Son, that whoever believes in Him should not perish but have everlasting life*" (John 3:16). He loved us so much that He sent His Son to die that painful and horrendous way to save us. Who was He saving? Sinners!

God, whom we cannot even begin to think or reason like, knows the end from the beginning, and in knowing that, He can direct our paths appropriately even when we don't have a clue what He is doing or why. He loves us so much that He wanted to give us a chance to live with Him forever and to shower us with grace. This is why He allowed Jesus to suffer and die in the horrible way He did. He needed a perfect, sinless sacrifice; one without blemish. Only God in human form could accomplish that. He did this to bridge the great chasm that separated God and man since the days of the Garden of Eden and the fall of man.

We see the love of God for us in Hebrews 2:9. "*But we see Jesus, who was made a little lower than the angels, for the suffering of death crowned with glory and honour, that He, by the grace of God, might taste death for everyone.*" Everyone! Grace is extended to all because of what Jesus did. God's loving grace toward us, and our disobedience, sent Christ to the cross. Therefore, each one of us held those spikes that were driven through Christ's hands and feet.

We all need to stop and take a personal inventory. It is important to step back and look at what we do and honestly ask why we do it. If we are not working towards pleasing God, but instead to get credit from our peers, church, and the world, our motives are wrong. Everything we do should be with a servant heart directed towards pleasing God alone. In doing this, our rewards will be stored up in heaven—just where He wants them to be (Matthew 6:19-21).

Just as God has extended grace to each one of us, sinful and carnal as we are, He expects us to extend that same grace to others and give them "room to grow." We all must be flexible and allow that room in each other's growth. God does love each of us so much. In His time, He will deal with every part of us, warts and all. We all have those spots that aren't so beautiful. We may try to hide them, but they are still there. When we stand before God, He sees the whole person, the outside and the inside. He knows all the good and bad, even the ugly. It's up to Him to judge us; it's not up to me to judge you, nor you to judge me (1 Corinthians 4:1-6).

Some will grow faster, and others slower. Some will develop differing opinions, but we need to be sensitive and give each other space. I believe many things are right and wrong, or black and white. Homosexuality, murder, greed, envy, jealousy, and lying are clearly sin, as the Bible points out, and are therefore wrong (1 Corinthians 6:9-10). However, there are some things that are not so black and white, and each person must seek God's will for their lives. Let me give you an example.

One night, my husband and I were watching TV together when the Lord spoke to my heart and said that I didn't need to be watching a certain program. Being who I am, I quickly announced to my husband that the program we were watching was inappropriate. He ignored me and continued watching. I got up in a huff and stormed out of the room. He didn't even notice my anger. He watched the show as I sat seething in the dining room, looking over a book I was in the process of reading.

Later, when I had a chance to cool off, we talked about it. He explained that it wasn't a "bad" program and after hearing him out and thinking about it, I had to agree.

After praying about it for some time, I realized there was no real reason for me to have expected him to turn the channel. The Lord convicted me—not him. Not everything that God reveals as good or bad for me is necessarily the same for everyone else. Sometimes it is just for me.

My personal desire and prayer to draw nearer to Him in specific ways means that His will for my life may be different than someone else's. He has a plan for my life and I need to be obedient in the things He requires of me. In turn, I need to extend grace to those who don't have the same convictions, without judgment.

Jesus requires each one of us to face Him in judgment alone. I will not have my husband or children, parents or friends to defend me on that day. I am responsible for every decision I make. Obedience or disobedience, it's all up to me. Jesus alone stands before me on that day. Knowing this, my heart and yours needs to be focused on the Lord and what He expects of each of us. He wants His grace to flow through us.

"*As each one has received a gift, minister it to one another, as good stewards of the manifold grace of God*" (1 Peter 4:10). By God's grace we are each given gifts, talents, and abilities. We are to use them to glorify God, not to raise ourselves above others or to feel puffed up and prideful. Something I have found in dealing with people is that sometimes gifts get buried, for fear of one kind or another. Sometimes it is fear of failure, sometimes a fear of success. Other times, it is a fear of ridicule or fear of losing a friend if you have a talent or ability that evokes some kind of envy or jealousy from a close person in your life.

Never allow anything to stand between you and God. *Never.* Not under any circumstance. God's grace is greater than anything. Do not allow fear to take over and destroy all that God has planned for you. The grace and blessings He will pour out because of obedience will far outweigh any reward on this earth.

This book had been in my notes for well over a year before I typed the first word. I felt the Lord urging me towards it, yet fear kept me from beginning. Then one night, after a very long and agonizing day in which everything seemed to go wrong and be painfully hard, I sat down to start. That had not been my plan. I had been planning to sit in my living room and have a pity party. All the frustration from the day and everything that had gone wrong had worn me down. I thought I should just let it all out.

As I walked towards the room, I passed the computer and that urging became overwhelming. So I gave in. I prayed and told the Lord that I felt there was not enough for me to write about, but if He had a book He wanted me to write, He would have to give me the words. As I am typing, a verse from 2 Corinthians comes to mind.

To give you background, Paul is speaking to Jesus about a thorn in his flesh he wanted removed. We aren't sure what the thorn was, but we do know that it was something he didn't want. He was in much distress and was praying for release from its hold on him. Jesus answered him saying, "*My grace is sufficient for you, for My strength is made perfect in weakness*" (2 Corinthians 12:9).

I am learning that His grace *is* sufficient. It is not always easy. When we release our worries and cares to Him, He can take the ugliest thing and make it beautiful. It will take time to trust in His promise of grace, but it is a free gift to all who will reach out and claim it for themselves. Just as the ballet dancer makes it look so easy, God will so easily extend grace to "the whosoever will."

CHAPTER SIX

THE PROMISE OF JOY

According to Merriam-Webster's Collegiate Dictionary, joy means "the emotion evoked by well-being, success or good fortune, or by the prospect of possessing what one desires."[2] This definition tells us that our joy is dependant on our material gains. Any time we depend on "things" to give us joy, we will quickly become disappointed.

Some people get a certain amount of satisfaction from spending money. The more they spend, the happier they are. That is, until the credit card bills come due.

Overspending and debt are huge problems in the family today. Money issues can tear families apart faster than almost anything else. Many times one spouse is a spender and the other is a saver. In the eyes of the saver,

[2] By permission. From *Merriam-Webster's Collegiate® Dictionary. 11th Edition*©2008 by Merriam-Webster, Incorporated (www.Merriam-Webster.com).

the spender is wasting money. In the eyes of the spender, the saver is just mean.

Television, catalogues, internet, and even friends can exacerbate the problem. The TV ad says, "You need it." The catalogue tells you, "You deserve it." A friend makes the comment, "I couldn't live without it!" In my house at any given time, there are at least thirty catalogues lying around here, there, and everywhere. Most of them are from different companies wanting to sell, sell, sell. It doesn't matter if you need it. They only need you to think you need it.

In the book of Matthew, Jesus warns us against these things. "*Do not lay up for yourselves treasures on earth, where moth and rust destroy and where thieves break in and steal; but lay up for yourselves treasures in heaven, where neither moth nor rust destroys and where thieves do not break in and steal. For where your treasure is, there your heart will be also*" (Matthew 6:19-21). If we focus on attaining more, more, more, we may lose focus on what truly counts in our lives. We all make decisions about what we will do each day. This is not any different. Our choice to put our treasures in Heaven will reward us fully one day. Jesus gives us a stern warning a little bit further on in that part of Scripture, saying, "*No one can serve two masters*" (Matthew 6:24). He wants us to make a choice to either live for Him or the world.

There is urgency for each of us to choose where our treasures will be. Many people have wealth and success, but are miserable. No amount of money can buy peace or joy. I have heard it said that there are two disappointments in life: the first, wanting something and not getting it, and the second, getting it.

How true that is! Stop and think about it for a moment. Think of all the things you have purchased over the years that you thought you couldn't live without. Maybe a pair of shoes you just had to have. What about in your kitchen cupboard? How many items do we buy thinking, "This will make that job so much easier"? Now think about how many of those items have either become dust collectors or just take up space. It might scare you. Many times we impulse buy, and then the moment we get home we wonder what we were thinking.

Joy is not dependant on the "things" you have on this earth. Joy is a gift that God wants to bless you with. Joy is one of the many promises He waits for you to choose. Yes, I said *choose.* Joy is a choice. As His child, He wants you to reach out and accept the joy He has promised you. Jesus spoke these words in John 15:11, "*These things I have spoken to you, that My joy may remain in you, and that your joy may be full.*"

If we look at the definition in the Student Bible Dictionary, we will see that joy has a very different meaning. It states that joy is "gladness, rejoicing (Ps. 16:11; Matt.2:10). An evidence of a Holy Spirit-filled life (Gal. 5:22)."[3] Galatians 5:22-23 mirrors that definition. "*But the fruit of the Spirit is love, joy, peace, longsuffering, kindness, goodness, faithfulness, gentleness, self control. Against such there is no*

[3] *The Student Bible Dictionary*. Barbour Publishing, Inc., Uhrichsville, Ohio. Used by permission.

law" (emphasis mine). Sounds like evidence of a Holy Spirit-filled life to me!

Joy is what the Father wants for us, His children. But how do we get there? First, we need to become connected with God. How? Seek His face. If you have not given your life to Him, re-read Chapter 2, The Promise of Salvation, and pray, giving your life over to Him so that you may enjoy the wonderful blessings He has in store for you.

Now that your life is His, I strongly suggest that you read and study the Bible. Don't just read your Bible, but memorize Scripture. Hide it in your heart so you have it firmly planted within you. Another helpful thing to do is to meditate on the Scriptures and allow God to reveal Himself and His will for your life through it.

Next, pray, pray, pray. You can set aside a time of prayer, but you may also pray when you are working or doing anything at any time. In your time of prayer, be sure to spend some of that time listening for His voice, not just talking. God speaks to us in a still, small voice. Quieting the heart and mind are necessary to hear Him and all that He is saying to each of us. (I know that I've said these things before. However, these steps are vital to our spiritual growth, so they deserve repeating.)

I remember a time in my Sunday school class when I experienced a prompting of the Spirit that would change my life. I was so overwhelmed, and even a bit disturbed by the prompting. So much so that, in the beginning, I disobeyed.

One of the men in my class was (and still is) a volunteer firefighter. He had been out on a call the night before. I heard the sirens blaring in the night. They woke me up and I could not return to sleep. I felt the need to pray. I prayed very simply. "Lord, I don't know who those sirens are for, but please be with them. Be with the firefighters who get out of their warm beds, even on cold winter nights, and fight fire. Father, protect them and the family they are going to help. You know the people in need. Protect them Lord, protect them Lord, protect them Lord." I drifted back to sleep with that prayer on my lips, on my heart, and in my soul.

I had no idea who I was asking God to protect that night, but the Holy Spirit was working within me. "*Likewise the Spirit also helps in our weaknesses. For we do not know what we should pray for as we ought, but the Spirit Himself makes intercession for us with groanings which cannot be uttered*" (Romans 8:26). He knew the prayer I needed to pray and who I was praying for, even though I was oblivious to the facts.

As my class drew to a close, he announced that the fire had been at my grandparents' house—about two miles from my own home. In that moment, I remembered praying the night before. I remembered not being able to sleep without praying first. The Spirit convicted me and I knew what I needed to do. I wrestled mentally with the thoughts that were so plain in front of me.

About eleven years before the fire, I walked out of my grandparents' home so offended that I vowed never to return. Hindsight proves that a small hurt can become an overwhelming monster in an instant. There is nothing Satan enjoys any more than seeing families ripped apart. I fell into the trap of holding a grudge all those years ago and God gave me the opportunity to right a wrong, but I was frozen with fear. What if they were too angry to accept me back into their family? What if I got a tongue-lashing to beat all? What if? What if? What if?

I knew that the Spirit was asking something of me. I even knew what it was. I am not proud to say that I was disobedient in the beginning, but I was. Fear can make you feel so empty and worthless. Satan is a master at filling us with fear, but when we lay fear at the foot of the cross and allow God to take it from us, He will replace that fear with peace and joy. What a great God we serve.

After a couple of days, fear still with me, I called our pastor and told him the barn that burned had belonged to my grandparents, and I asked him what I should do. I felt that our pastor should have a better connection with the Lord than I did. I felt that if he gave me advice, I could follow it and somehow get out of this burden from the Holy Spirit that was so heavy. I prayed that He would tell me I was justified in my anger and didn't have to do anything any differently. Most of all, I was looking for a way out of the prompting I knew I was given by the Holy Spirit.

After explaining my history with them (in abbreviated form), I asked, "What do you think I should do?" His answer was simple. "Why don't you make up a basket of goodies and take it to them?" I was in shock! Of all the things he could have said. Why, why did he have to say that?! Days before, as I had stood in front of my class, I heard the initial prompting of the Spirit speak clearly to my heart, "Make them up a basket of goodies like you used to and take it to them." Right then and there, I knew I had been severely disobedient.

I was upset with my pastor because I wanted a way out, which he didn't give me. The anger I felt at that point in time was coming from my own sense of disobedience. I knew what I needed to do, yet I ignored it and tried to justify it away. Disobedience gives way to sin, and sin gives way to distance from God. Shame began to flood me. I could have allowed the shame and guilt I was feeling to overwhelm me, but I didn't. This time, I refused to allow Satan to win. I prayed and asked God's forgiveness, and set to work on the goodies.

As I baked cookies, I prayed for God to go before me and prepare their hearts and mine. I went one day and no one was home. The next day I went, it was Christmas Eve. The closer I got to their driveway, the more fearful I became. My adrenaline was pumping and I wanted to drive by, but I knew what I needed to do. I sent up an emergency prayer. "Please Lord, be with me and guide me. I pray for You to open their hearts and mine. Amen."

It had been such a long time. Would they know me? Would they answer the door? Fear tore through my body like a freight train. It seemed that it would be so much easier to just keep holding that grudge than to forgive it and let it go. Seconds felt like an eternity as I applied the brake and put the van in park. I opened the van door and my Grampie met me in the doorway.

He embraced me and I thought he would never let me go. All fear dissolved and joy swept through my body and soul. As he hugged me, he praised God and it overwhelmed me to the point of tears. After a quick talk, we agreed to leave the past right where the past belonged and move ahead, to be a family again.

When I saw my Grammie, the greeting was the same. Love and forgiveness. Forgiveness at its best. The joy I felt in that moment was incredible. I knew instantly that they both still loved me. Most of all, I knew that God loves me so much. He wants to give me joy in ways I cannot even begin to imagine. All of this joy came out of a pile of ashes and the prompting of the Holy Spirit. When we step back and allow God to work, we will see miracles. Lives can be transformed and healing that does not seem possible will occur. God can mend the heart and fill it with joy.

Sometimes those promptings seem superfluous or irrelevant, but it may just be a simple test of obedience. The Holy Spirit may prompt you to do something as simple as making muffins for your neighbour or placing a call to a friend who is having a difficult time. God will sometimes ask us to do things we feel are unimportant or seem too hard. But when we are in His will, He will bless us in ways we cannot begin to imagine. We can find excuses or reason it away, but God wants us to do it when He asks. Don't be like me and try to wriggle your way out of it. Look at the blessings my family and I would have missed.

If I hadn't followed His will for my life, I would still be without grandparents and my children might never have met their great-grandparents. What a huge blessing He has poured out on me, though I don't feel I deserve it. He wants to bless us through whatever He sends our way. It may seem impossible at the time, but remember, "*I can do all things through Christ who strengthens me*" (Philippians 4:13). I can, and so can you. Don't try to do it alone. Give it to God, be obedient, and watch what He can do. He wants to bless us with joy through the circumstances that come our way.

I am learning the importance of following His instruction when He gives them to me. Not that I'm perfect. I'm far from it. I do make mistakes, but I am learning. God wants to know that we love Him and that we will obey Him in all things in His time.

In Matthew, Jesus is teaching His disciples when He is asked which is the greatest commandment. "*Jesus said to him, 'You shall love the Lord your God with all your heart, with all your soul, and with all your mind*'" (Matthew 22:37). We will never be able to obtain true joy without Him. Joy that comes from the Lord is an ever-filling joy.

It is important to give Him all our burdens and allow Him to replace those burdens with His joy. We also need to give our successes to Him and allow Him to fill us. If we fill ourselves with the praise and flattery of the world, there will be no room for Him. Being filled by God will keep us afloat and level—not bobbing and sinking like a capsized ship at sea.

We serve the same God today that the Israelites served in the Old Testament. Isaiah 51:11 says "*They shall obtain joy and gladness; sorrow and sighing shall flee away.*" God wanted to fill His people with joy in that day and He wants to fill us right now. True joy comes straight out of

Heaven from God. It flows directly into our hearts by way of Jesus Christ through the Holy Spirit within.

True joy is knowing that you will be with Him through eternity. This knowledge allows you to confidently share that truth, unmoved by the obstacles in your way. It is a quiet reassurance that you will be there in His presence without sorrow or sighing, crying or dying.

In Psalm 40:1-3, we see David waiting. "*I waited patiently for the Lord; he turned to me and heard my cry. He lifted me out of the slimy pit, out of the mud and mire; he set my feet on a rock and gave me a firm place to stand. He put a new song in my mouth, a hymn of praise to our God. Many will see and fear and put their trust in the Lord*" (NIV).

In this passage, God heard David's cry and then we see that he received three things of benefit. First, after crying out and waiting, God came to David's rescue. He lifted David out of the deep despair he was in. Second, God proceeded to set his feet on a rock. Rocks are steady and firm. You can count on them not to move. God gave David a firm place to stand, something that he could depend on. Finally, God gave David joy. He put a song in his mouth. Whatever we go through, God can give us joy.

Some blessings only come after waiting, but they are well worth the wait. If you are in a dry time of waiting, realize that God does test us through it, but He never leaves us, no matter what it "feels" like. Don't give up. Continue praying as David did. God is faithful and He will come to you, but you may have to wait on His timing, which can be very difficult.

During his wait time, David prayed (Psalm 5:3). We can learn a lot from that. If we pray and serve God while we are waiting, joy will fill us. Joy is a decision. We can decide to be miserable or we can decide to find the good in whatever life dishes out to us. Paul shares his contentment with life in Philippians 4:11, *"For I have learned in whatever state I am, to be content."* Joy follows contentment. We need to spend our time doing what God has placed us on earth to do. If you aren't sure what that is yet, pray expecting God to hear and answer you. In the meantime, why not lend a helping hand?

Nothing makes a person feel any better than to help another person in need. If you have never reached out to give someone a hand, try it. It will fill your heart with a joy that no amount of money can buy. The look in a person's face who is hungry, whom you give a sandwich to; a hurting person, who you take your time to listen to even though you may not know them; the frustrated mom at the grocery store with screaming children, who you smile at and reassure that it's okay. We can help fill others with joy by the way we treat them. God loves it when we are uplifting and encouraging to one another.

Grace can be extended in so many ways, to so many people. Giving is much more rewarding than receiving. Pray and let the Lord lead you in mighty and powerful ways. Follow the promptings of the Spirit and don't forget to thank Him for the joy you feel when you have been obedient. If you've been disobedient as I have, don't allow Satan to beat you down anymore. Ask God for His forgiveness and move forward—being sensitive and prayerful to whatever the Spirit asks of you. Prepare to be filled with the joy of the Lord.

CHAPTER SEVEN

THE PROMISE OF CONNECTION WITH GOD THROUGH PRAYER

Prayer can be such a wonderful experience. It can also be an extremely intimidating, negative experience, especially in a group. I remember my first prayer meeting. It was very awkward for me. I wanted so badly to pray, yet fear kept me from praying in front of everyone who was there. I felt overwhelmed and guilty.

I remember sitting there and looking around at the faces in that meeting. All of them had been Christians much longer than I. I heard some of them pray on other occasions and wondered how inadequate my prayers would sound when weighed against theirs. I also felt ashamed at the fact that I had never attended a prayer meeting before in my life. Looking back, I do not remember it as a positive experience. I did, however, pray in my heart with them, but spoke not an audible word.

I forced myself to go to the prayer meeting regularly, because I knew that I needed to develop a deep and lasting relationship with Jesus to enable me to work through a lot of the "junk" I was carrying around with me. Though the first experience was not a great one, I knew in my heart that I needed to go. Finally, what I was dreading finally became reality. The pastor asked me to pray.

In my simple, awkward way, I prayed. Instead of my mind being focused on the Lord that day, I spent most of my time worried about what the people around me were thinking about my "lame" way of praying. Some of them were (and still are) such awesome and eloquent prayer warriors. In my mind, I wondered if my prayers mattered at all. I couldn't imagine how God could understand anything I was trying to say, because I didn't have a clue myself.

As well as attending prayer meetings, I continued praying at home on a regular basis in my quiet time. Then something happened. I began to sense God acknowledging and sometimes even answering my prayers. I found the time I spent with Him was such a wonderful, peaceful, tranquil time. The time I spent (and continue to spend) in His presence recharged me and gave me a knowledge that He loved and cared for me. My relationship with Him has grown deeper and stronger ever since.

Though my relationship was developing with the Lord, I would still experience fear in a prayer group setting. The fear would creep in and leap on me out of the darkness and pull me down. With the fear came feelings of inadequacy and foolishness. Paul tells us in the book of 2 Timothy that these feelings are not from God. "*For God has not given us a spirit of fear, but of power and of love and of a sound mind*" (2 Timothy 1:7).

I hadn't yet understood this truth. God doesn't make us fearful and He doesn't want us to live in fear. Satan was hard at work trying to discourage me from connecting with God through prayer in a group. Much happens when we pray in a group setting. Matthew 18:20 gives us direction. Jesus is speaking and says, "*For where two or three are gathered together in My name, I am there in the midst of them.*" Jesus comes into our midst when we gather together and pray. There is incredible power and strength in collective prayer.

One day in my Bible reading time, I came across a passage that said, "*And when you pray, you shall not be like the hypocrites*" (Matthew 6:5). After studying that passage of Scripture, I realized that my simple prayers were okay, but my worry and wonder about what other people thought made my prayers like those of the hypocrites. I was so concerned about what other people thought that I couldn't focus on Jesus, who I was praying to. We pray to the Lord. Our focus should be on Him. We should not pray to impress others. If we do, it's time to check our priorities. After I realized what I had been doing, I prayed and asked God to forgive me and to give me strength to focus only on Him in my prayer time; whether alone or in a group.

God asks us to pray our hearts to Him, to pour out our lives and be honest in our reverence, our worship, and in our requests. I don't have to sound like a theology student or a pastor. I need to sound like me. The same applies to you. Fancy, biblical, or encyclopaedic words are not necessary. If that type of language is natural for you, great, but it is not required. All that is required is an honest, transparent heart that loves the Lord with all it is.

I thank the Lord that He sees the heart (1 Samuel 16:7). He knows all that is truly going on in each one of our lives and in our hearts. We cannot hide anything good or bad from Him. He sees it all.

It is easy to get caught up in the thought that everything we pray to God needs to be nice and neat and that we need to have a pasted smile on our face. That would be wonderful, if it were a true description of your feelings. Sometimes, though, that is not the case. There are times in our lives when we are angry, frustrated, hurt, or disappointed. Our lives can feel like they are unravelling. Job loss, death, illness, and relationship problems can be overwhelming.

In those times, it is okay to be honest in our prayers to the Lord. Remember, Jesus knows your pain. He went through more pain than we can ever begin to imagine (Hebrews 4:15). We can be honest with Him and He will continue to love us. Psalm 55, 69, 88, and 102 are wonderful examples of pouring out an honest heart to God. Yes, Jesus desires our praise and adoration, but He also wants our honesty. Let's face it: the heart is not always happy, joyful, and full of praise.

Prayer needs to be an honest exchange with the Lord. He knows every part of you, including your thoughts and feelings. Open your heart and pour it all out before Him. When we finally do, then and only then can He bring healing to our lives. We mustn't dwell on the negative things, but bring them to the Lord, lay them at His feet, and leave them there. Once we leave it with Him, He can transform the ugly into something beautiful.

Prayer has been such a promise to me. I have seen God move in times that were absolutely, positively impossible. I have seen prayer bring a man back from the brink of death. I've seen Him provide when there was no logical way possible. I have seen God move in very unmistakable ways. Prayer is the greatest overcomer. God is so good and He hears and answers prayer.

Paul instructs us to "*pray without ceasing*" (1 Thessalonians 5:17). Our job is to pray, have faith that God is able, and then allow Him time and space to work it all out. In the book of 1 Kings 8:56-61, Solomon blesses the assembly. In verse 59, he says, "*And may these words of mine, with which I have made supplication before the Lord, be near the Lord our God day and night, that He may maintain the cause of His servant and the cause of His people Israel, as each day may require*" (emphasis mine).

God will keep our prayers near Him. This is a wonderful prayer to pray. Ask the Lord to keep those precious cares near Him day and night. It will be amazing to see what He will do when we trust completely, releasing our cares, worries, families, and loved ones into His care. I imagine it as putting all that "stuff" in a big box, tying it with a beautiful ribbon, and laying it at the throne of grace, at Jesus' feet, like a present.

For me, I have had a hard time giving up my worries and cares. Once I began to understand this passage, I developed a trust in Jesus that He truly loves and cares for me. He is concerned about my concerns. I don't have to carry all those burdens. He will take them and make them beautiful in His time (Ecclesiastes 3:11).

Training ourselves to be consistent in our prayer life is so important. It may not always be fun or easy, but the rewards will be worth it. We exercise and train our bodies. How much more should we train our spiritual lives, which will go on for all eternity? (1 Timothy 4:8) Our prayers should always be in line with God's Word. He left us an example in the Lord's Prayer (Matthew 6:9-13).

He will never give us anything that will be harmful or detrimental to us. We may pray for a million dollars and He may give it to us. But, He may not. "'*For I know the plans I have for you,' declares the Lord, 'plans to prosper you and not to harm you, plans to give you hope and a future*'" (Jeremiah 29:11, NIV). He knows what is best. Always.

In my own life, I have seen prayer heal a relationship that was broken for more than ten years. It took two years of prayer with others praying with me for things to begin. God began to work in my heart and change the way I related to my past and allowed me to forgive—truly forgive. During that time of prayer, it sometimes felt as though nothing would ever change. I was fortunate to have a close prayer partner who would give me godly advice and Scripture to help me in my private prayer time so I would know God's will for the situation.

When we pray, it gives God the chance to tell us whether we are in His will or not. In 2 Samuel 7, David wants to build a house for the Lord. He is feeling a bit guilty about having a home while the Lord resides in a tent. He speaks with Nathan, the prophet, about his concerns and Nathan gives him the go ahead. That night, God spoke to Nathan and instructed him to tell David no.

Many times our intentions and thoughts may be good, but it may not be what God wants us to do. We have to be responsible to "*lead every thought and purpose away captive into the obedience of Christ*" (2 Corinthians 10:5, AMP). Our ideas, dreams, thoughts, and everything else included. Good ideas aren't always of God. That's why prayer is so important. He will give us guidance and direction for our lives when we truly seek Him and listen.

Prayer can open the floodgates of Heaven and allow God to pour His blessings upon us. God cannot work in our lives if we don't pray and invite Him to do the work that is necessary. It is our prayers that allow Him to work and reveal His power and dominion over our lives. Many times, I am tempted to do it alone. But I've been there. Alone is not the place to be. The results aren't that great. I trust Him enough to allow Him to direct my life. It can still be hard, but with the power of Heaven behind you, how can you lose?

CHAPTER EIGHT

PROMISES CONCERNING SPIRITUAL WARFARE

The battle of the mind is probably the greatest battle of all. What happens in our minds plays out in our lives by the way we live. Some of what happens in our minds we can learn to control. The Bible is very clear in its instruction to us about our thoughts and how to deal with them. The latter part of 2 Corinthians 10:5 states, "*We lead every thought into captivity to the obedience of Christ*" (AMP). This means that everything we do, and even what we think, should be in God's hands. He is our leader and we should follow Him according to His ways.

I've been told that for every negative thought or word, one must say at least ten positive thoughts or words just to cancel out the negative one. That does not put you on the positive side, but only serves to keep you from falling into the negatives. After you cancel out that negative, you must continue to repeat positive comments and positive thoughts until you look at situations and yourself with a more positive outlook. Ephesians 4:29 talks about how we should speak. "*Do not let any unwholesome talk come out of your mouths, but only what is helpful for building others up according to their needs, that it may benefit those who listen*" (NIV). We need to feed ourselves and others with positive comments if we want to become positive.

Satan can't wait to see someone degrading themselves. "I'm worthless. Nobody loves me. I'm ugly. I'm stupid." These comments may be some of the things you think or say to and about yourself on a regular basis. If so, that steady diet of negativity will get you nowhere fast. Just as a stone sinks to the bottom of the lake, so will your self-worth.

Satan loves it. Revelation 12:10 tells us he is "*the accuser of our brothers*"(NIV). He wants you to believe his lies about you and your Christian brothers and sisters. If you will listen to him and his lies, he will be more than happy to join you in your pity party. He will even bring some more of your faults to your attention so you can really do a number on yourself. Don't buy into the lies. God doesn't make any junk. Remember, He *did* make you.

If this is the way you communicate with yourself, you will be fighting a spiritual battle that Satan wants to win. Remember, being a Christian does not insulate you from Satan's attacks, but it does ensure that you have the power of Heaven behind you if you will humble yourself, seek forgiveness, and ask for the Lord's help (2 Chronicles 7:14). Many battles have been won because of the power *of* and persistence *in* prayer. When we pray, we open the floodgates of Heaven and allow God's blessings to spill over onto us.

Does that mean that every time we pray, we will get a miracle? No. Does that mean that we should expect one? Why not! Pray, expecting God to move. He is capable. He is able. However, God does see the big picture, He knows it all (Revelation 22:13).

There was a time when I was praying for a certain situation in my life to be resolved and God was not answering me in the way I thought He should. I stopped praying about it and started asking Him why. Why, Lord? Why don't You fix this? You, who hung the stars in the sky? You, who created everything we see out of nothing? Why, God, why?

After a time of pleading with Him, in my mind's eye I could see this path in front of me. It was winding, dipping, and turning every which way. Then off to the right side was another path. The left side showed another. Above me was yet another. There were paths everywhere. They seemed to intertwine at different points, then veer sharply away. The paths continued on, moving this way and that.

Then somewhere in the quiet of my soul I could feel a strong, deep conviction of the Lord, telling me that only He knew the outcome of those paths that were before me. Each one belonged to a different person. At different times, we are in contact with another person and that is when they come together. When we are away from them, our paths veer away. The important thing I learned was this: only He knows each curve and where it will take each person involved.

A flood of peace flowed over my soul that only God can give. I felt a deep desire to be in His will and I was able to give over to Him the situation that had been disturbing me. I felt a strong conviction to box it up, tie it with a bow, and lay it at His feet, allowing Him to do whatever it took to arrive at His perfect will. Again I prayed, but this time I asked for His mercy and forgiveness, thanking Him for showing me this truth.

Sometimes our wants and wishes don't exactly mould to what God wants for us. Many times, like children, we as adults think we need something so badly. Your thought may be, "If I could just have (you fill in the blank), then I would be happy. I would never ask for another thing in my whole life." But just like a child, it is either never enough or it doesn't bring the happiness, peace, or joy you thought it would. God knows our needs, wants, and wishes. If we would allow Him to, He would bless us beyond what our wildest imagination could dream up (Philippians 4:19). It isn't easy to submit to the will of God, but the peace and rewards that come from it far outweigh the cost.

If Satan can make you believe his lies, that you are all of those negative things, then you are no threat to him. It can be very depressing to have negative thoughts and emotions, and they can overtake you if not kept in check. We have to maintain control over our mind. Learning to focus on positive things is important. Paul instructs us in Philippians 4:8 on how to focus on the good. "*Finally, brethren, whatever things are true, whatever things are noble, whatever things are just, whatever things are pure, whatever things are lovely, whatever things are of good report, if there is any virtue and if there is anything praiseworthy—meditate on these things.*" What a wonderful way to adjust our thinking! Focusing on positive, lovely things will keep us from sinking in the muck.

Personally, prayer and reading my Bible have made an incredible difference. I used to live in a deep, dark pit. I decorated it and thought it was pretty nice. I was comfortable there. I wasn't happy, but it was familiar. I lived a life of negativity and depression. Through it all, Jesus was there, patiently waiting for me. He is such a gentleman. He will never push Himself on you. He will not force the issue. However, He will wait and be there for you the moment you choose Him. Jesus heard my heart-cry and reached way down and pulled me from the darkness and into the light. He is waiting for you (Revelation 3:20). Just say the word.

One point that I would like to make here is that I am well aware that depression is a very real disease and there are many people who need medication to cope with it on a day to day basis. That is a very different situation than what I am talking about. If you are on any type of medication for any type of depression, do not, I repeat, do not go off your medication without permission from your doctor. There are serious cases in which medication is needed. I am not saying that you should be able to control your mind to that extent.

What I am saying is that negative self-talk is a dangerous road to tread on. God made us all "*in His own image*" (Genesis 1:27). Therefore you are made just the way you should be. A billboard sign on a church I saw some time ago was, "God loves you just the way you are, but refuses to let you stay that way." That quote stuck with me. I thought about it for some time and even argued that it was wrong. Over time, God revealed His truth to me. What it means is that, although God does love me (and you) just the way I am, He wants me to grow and change to be more like Him each and every day. Isn't that awesome?

The more I study about who God is, the more I realize this is true. Yes, He loves me. No question. But He wants more and better for me than I can ever imagine. He wants the same for you. His love is so amazing. Once He touches your life, you will never be the same (2 Corinthians 5:17). There have been changes in my heart and in my life that I would never have believed possible just a few short years ago. God is powerful!

Our thoughts can defeat us in a split second if we allow them to. Our thoughts can also lead us in the right direction if our focus is in line with God's will for our lives. In our attempt to live life, we can sometimes become so consumed with "I want" or "I need" that we forget the bigger picture. Satan loves for us to show the weaknesses of self-centeredness and selfishness. He will cheer us on as we become consumed with self while the distance between ourselves and God becomes so great that we can no longer hear what God is saying.

In the book of Ephesians, Paul instructs us to prepare each day for the spiritual battlefront that awaits us. "*Therefore put on the full armor of God, so that when the day of evil comes, you may be able to stand your ground, and after you have done everything, to stand. Stand firm then, with the belt of truth buckled around your waist, with the breastplate of righteousness in place, and with your feet fitted with the readiness that comes from the gospel of peace. In addition to all this, take up the shield of faith, with which you can extinguish all the flaming arrows of the evil one. Take the helmet of salvation and the sword of the Spirit, which is the word of God*" (Ephesians 6:13-17, NIV).

Each and every day we have the option to stay in our bedclothes or get dressed. We decide what we will wear. When we get up to begin our day, it would be a great idea to "put on" our spiritual armour as well. Prayer will help us gird ourselves in spiritual armour and prepare us for the day. Let's just take a quick look at each of these pieces of spiritual armour.

The Belt of Truth. The belt is the foundational piece in your armour. One thing Satan does very well is lie. He can make things sound and appear true. 2 Corinthians 11:14 tells us, "*And no wonder! For Satan himself transforms himself into an angel of light.*" Just because it sounds like the truth doesn't make it so. Be aware that a half-lie is still a lie. Your Bible will never contradict God, but Satan will. If you are unsure, check God's Word.

The Breastplate of Righteousness. Satan attacks our hearts: "You're worthless, you'll never amount to anything, nobody likes you," and so on. These are hurtful comments, lies that we can easily believe if we haven't covered our hearts with the breastplate of righteousness. Jesus came to this earth, died, and rose again to make us acceptable before God and not even Satan can take that away from us.

Footgear of Peace. Everyone deserves to hear the message of Jesus. Satan wants to discourage us, but with the footgear of peace we can be confident that our spreading the Good News is never a waste of time.

Shield of Faith. In the beginning of our Christian walk, our faith may be small. As our knowledge and faith grow, so does our shield. The more we know about God, the more faith we have and the better able we are to protect ourselves from Satan's fiery darts.

Helmet of Salvation. Satan wants to discourage us so we will doubt God and His promises. With the helmet of salvation, we can be assured of the work Jesus did on the cross all those years ago. He loves us. Our salvation is assured because of it. Nothing Satan says or does can change it. Our responsibility is to stand firm in our faith in Jesus Christ.

Sword of the Spirit. Our Bible is our only offensive weapon. There will probably be times when reciting Scripture aloud will be the only way to stop Satan's attacks. Memorizing Scripture is so important for this purpose. If you have the Scripture in your heart, you can deflect the enemy's attacks. Claim God's promises, His truths, His love, and Satan will flee (James 4:7).

We have all the protection we need. God has given us His Word, timeless and truthful, for God never changes. He is the same God He was during the time of Moses and so He will be for all eternity. We can count on His protection and love if we will trust and have faith in Him.

Satan attacks with lies that look and sound like truth. So how can we know the difference? Knowing God, claiming His promises, and remembering what He has already done for you are great ways to start. Each day before you get out of bed, you can put on the "armour of God," knowing that there is a spiritual battle to be fought each and every day.

Circumstances in our lives, like a sick child, cancer diagnosis, death of a loved one, or job loss can be sudden and overwhelming. Be aware that Satan enjoys whispering lies in your ear when these things come up against you. That is why it is so important to know God's promises for you. Put His words in your heart and mind. Psalm 27:1 is simple to learn and can help through so many trials. "*The Lord is my light and my salvation—whom shall I fear?*" (NIV) Another that is true and comforting is, "*If God is for us, who can be against us?*" (Romans 8:31, NIV) Find some passages from the Bible that personally speak to you and place them in your heart so that you will be able to use the sword of the Spirit when the time comes.

Most of all, have faith. Know that God knows the end from the beginning. It is all in His hands. We must look to God first, seeing the circumstances through Him, and know that He is in control. After we do that, we just might find ourselves in the true purpose of it all—God's will. In Scripture, you will never find a quote that says it will be easy, but you will find, "*I will never leave you nor forsake you*" (Hebrews 13:5).

CHAPTER NINE

GOD'S PROMISE OF PROTECTION

One of the first questions we ask as we are growing up and preparing to move out on our own is, "Where will I live?" We all seek the protection that a roof over our heads provides. Some homes may not look like much and others may be mansions, but we want to know that we have shelter from the elements. We seek protection.

Whenever we love someone, we have an instinctive sense of protection. We want to protect, at any cost, at any risk. We feel a strong sense of duty to protect. Whether that love is for a kitten, a friend, or a child, the responsibility to protect them is within us. We are all programmed to have a desire to protect anyone or anything that in our eyes is more vulnerable than ourselves.

That built-in desire comes from God, who deeply desires to protect us. God's desire to save and protect us sent Jesus to the cross at Calvary all those years ago. Jesus bore the burden of all sinners, past, present, and future (Hebrews 9:28). He will never again have to go on that cross. He defeated death and the grave to give us protection. Psalm 139:5 says, "*You have hedged me behind and before, And laid Your hand upon me.*" God fences us in. It reminds me of an invisible force-field. His protection covers us day and night, year in and year out.

That said, I know many people who have put their faith in Him and still encountered struggles. God never said it would be easy. There are times when we must go through some struggles to move ahead in our spiritual walk with Him. He knows the way. A friend of mine once said, "God doesn't have a back-up plan; He has a plan."

Those can be tough words to swallow. It has taken me some years to truly understand and acknowledge the truth in those words, but God is the same God He has always been. When Jesus prayed in the Garden of Gethsemane, He prayed to God, saying, "*Father, if it is Your will, take this cup away from Me; nevertheless not My will, but Yours, be done*" (Luke 22:42).

God didn't have a back-up plan for Jesus, but Jesus prayed for God's will, asking if it could be changed. When we go through struggles, it is easy to look around and see someone else's blessing and be envious, but try to keep in mind what Jesus had to go through. He had all of Heaven waiting on Him. He could have been rescued at a moment's notice, but He knew the requirement for our redemption and He was willing to pay the price.

In the book of Deuteronomy, God makes a promise of protection to Israel:

"When you go out to battle against your enemies, and see horses and chariots and people more numerous than you, do not be afraid of them; for the Lord your God is with you, who brought you up from the land of Egypt. So it shall be, when you are on the verge of battle, that the priest shall approach and speak to the people. And he shall say to them,

'Hear, O Israel: Today you are on the verge of battle with your enemies. Do not let your heart faint, do not be afraid, and do not tremble or be terrified because of them; for the Lord your God is He who goes with you, to fight for you against your enemies, to save you" (Deuteronomy 20:1-4).

This promise of protection is very specific in how God protected the Israelites during wartime. He wanted them to be comforted and confident in the power God had over His people. The promise God made to the Israelites is a promise we can also claim. We need not be fearful *"for the battle is the Lord's"* (1 Samuel 17:47). Does that mean that we will never be fearful of anything? I doubt it, but it is possible that in times of fear and doubt, looking to God will give us, *"the peace of God, which surpasses all understanding"* (Philippians 4:7). The logical part of the mind is hard to overcome, but not impossible. With faith and God's help, all things are possible.

If we could see the power of Heaven we have behind us, we might be more confident in the God we serve. However, God wants our faith to be put in Him because of what we know about Him. If we look at 2 Kings 6:16-17, we will see the truth about the God we serve. *"So he answered, 'Do not fear, for those who are with us are more than those who are with them.' And Elisha prayed, and said, 'Lord, I pray, open his eyes that he may see.' Then the Lord opened the eyes of the young man, and he saw. And behold, the mountain was full of horses and chariots of fire all around Elisha."*

The truth was revealed in an awesome, powerful way. He saw God's mighty army there before him. The protection we have is with us, only we do not have the privilege to see what is going on. If we do not see God working in our lives, it may not be that He is not working, but that we don't have the spiritual eyesight to recognize it. Faith is key. Our decision to believe God's Word is totally up to us. He gave us free will so that we could make our own choice to choose or reject Him. The right choice leads to a life of freedom, while the wrong choice leads to a life of bondage.

Everything we do is a choice. Personally, I have a love-hate relationship with free will. I love the fact that God loves us enough to give us a choice. However, I hate the fact that I sometimes have so much trouble making the right choices. One thing is for certain, though: God's protection is with us. We may make mistakes, but when we are tuned in to God's voice, He is quick to let us know right from wrong. When we make a mistake, we will know it. Making mistakes is not a big deal if you repent and truly seek forgiveness. As soon as the Spirit convicts you, pray with your whole heart immediately to avoid guilt and shame. Remember to ask the Holy Spirit to guide you not to repeat your mistake.

God does allow things to come into our lives that are not desirable. Job is a perfect example of this. *"So Satan answered the Lord and said, 'Does Job fear God for nothing? Have You not made a hedge around him, around his household, and around all that he has on every side? You have blessed the work of his hands, and his possessions have increased in the land. But now, stretch out Your hand and touch all that he has, and he will surely curse You to Your face!' And the Lord said to Satan, 'Behold, all that he has is in your power; only do not lay a hand on his person"* (Job 1:9-12; for a full account of Job's life, read the book of Job).

This passage of Scripture teaches us some important truths. First, we are never sent anything that God hasn't allowed. If so, Satan wouldn't have needed God's permission to "attack" Job. Second, we know that God will protect us because He told Satan that he could not "lay a hand on his *person*." God is the same today as He was when Job was alive. He does not want us to suffer; however, there are times that suffering is the only way to make someone see the truth.

God promises to *"never leave you nor forsake you"* (Hebrews 13:5). What a promise! Wherever you are, you are being protected by God the Father, God the Son, and God the Holy Spirit. He loves you so much.

One day, I realized this truth firsthand. Our family was getting ready to go away to the city for an appointment. The drive from our home into the city is about three hours. I am a very organized person and I much prefer to be early, rather than just be on time.

We got our daughters and ourselves ready to go out the door. As we were headed out, I checked my watch. *Good*, I thought. *We should be early*. Just before the door closed behind us, the phone rang. My husband wanted to check it in case it was important. He answered the phone and the minutes rolled by. By the second, I became more and more frustrated. All I could think about was getting to that appointment on time. After what seemed like forever, we finally got on our way. Driving along the road, we came to what looked like roadwork. We waited and I became agitated.

As we were waved through, we saw a car down over the bank being towed up to the side of the road. There were police cars and ambulances. It was a bad crash. At that moment, I thanked God for holding us up. We may have been in the middle of it if we hadn't had that call when we did. God will use anything to protect us. Sometimes it is as simple as a phone call that seems like an inconvenience.

Now when I'm tempted to be frustrated by the little inconveniences of life, I try to remember that day and God's protection on our family. If we had left on time, we may have been right in the center of that accident, which could have been fatal. God's hand is always upon us. I love Psalm 91 and the way it so beautifully describes God's protection. The first four verses are so wonderfully written. As you read it, picture it in your mind. One can actually envision God's protection.

> "He who dwells in the secret place of the Most High shall abide under the

> shadow of the Almighty. (...) He shall cover you with His feathers, and under His wings you shall take refuge; His truth *shall be your* shield and buckler." (Psalm 91:1,4)

Can you feel the love of the Father? Can you feel the warmth of His shadow? Do you feel the comfort of His protection? God loves His children and He desires to keep us protected. Will you allow His truth to be your shield? Claim His promise of protection now, trusting that what He says is true, and allow His ways to become your ways.

CHAPTER TEN

FORGIVENESS

Forgiveness. I chose to put this chapter at the end of the book not because it is least important, but because of my past struggles with the concept of forgiving. The first time I read a chapter in a book about forgiveness, I kept reading that word over and over again. *Forgiveness.*

It was like a needle on a scratched record that kept playing the same word over and over, forgiveness, forgiveness, forgiveness... Adrenaline began to pump. My breathing became shallow and rapid. It was crazy. My body was responding to such a loving word in a terribly negative way. I glanced down at that word one more time in an effort to begin reading, but I couldn't get past it. I wanted to scream. Promptly, I threw the book onto the floor and jumped all over it.

Forgive. I wasn't going to forgive. Why should I? I had been hurt. I needed to protect myself. Forgiveness was the furthest thing from my mind. I reached down to the floor, picked up the book, and stashed it away so I wouldn't have to think about it. My feeling (at that time) was that if God loves me and truly knows my hurt, surely He wouldn't expect me to forgive. I truly believed that He only expected forgiveness in certain circumstances. I was of the opinion that forgiveness was optional.

I wasn't ready to consider the fact that I had to forgive. As a girl, I was taught "Hurt me once, shame on you. Hurt me twice, shame on me." In other words, if someone hurt me more than once, it was my own fault for letting them. Learning that taught me to build walls around myself so no one could ever hurt me again. Maybe you feel the same way. Maybe your experience with hurt is so bad that you think you will never be able to forgive or trust again.

One thing I have come to realize is this: we are all human. At some point, even "good Christians" are going to hurt one another and get hurt. It is not intentional, but it does happen. Far too often, I might add. James tells us, "The tongue also is a fire, a world of evil among the parts of the body. It corrupts the whole person, sets the whole course of his life on fire, and is itself set on fire by hell" (James 3:6, NIV).

James shines some truth on the abilities (or may we say, disabilities) of the tongue. As quickly as a small spark can destroy a forest, so can the tongue destroy if not trained properly. Let's be honest about it. Much of the time, hurts happen because the tongue has been let loose. James 3:8 says, *"But no man can tame the tongue. It is a restless evil, full of deadly poison"* (NIV).

You may be saying, "Why bother then? I haven't got a chance at being in control of what I say, so why bother even thinking about it?" Please don't think such things. The wonderful thing is that we have the ability, with the power of the Holy Spirit, to train the tongue. David prays an incredible prayer to help train the fiery tongue. Psalm 141:3 says, *"Set a guard over my mouth, O Lord; keep watch over the door of my lips"* (NIV). What a fabulous verse for us to learn! We can recite this prayer at any time, in any situation. I know using this verse has helped me keep my lips closed when I have truly wanted to lose my temper.

A gift my husband has that I would love to have, naturally, is the gift of turning everything around to see the good in it. He doesn't offend easily. He doesn't have to deal with the forgiveness issue on an ongoing basis, because he sees the good in everything. I have come home many times, offended by something someone has said or done. Ranting and raving, I will tell him what happened. Somehow, he can always twist it around to find some kind of good in it.

In the past, I always expected the worst, so that's what I got. I expected people to offend me, so they did. However, learning to hear people's comments objectively, rather than personally, makes all the difference. Just as expecting the worst can lead to the worst, expecting good can result in good things happening. Many times, it is a matter of perspective.

It is amazing how when we decide to look for the good, we will have the ability to find it. This is not something that can be done on one's own. Being able to find good in all things is a God-given gift. If it is unnatural for you, do not be discouraged. With training, it can be achieved. The latter part of Matthew 19:26 is very close to my heart. Jesus is talking and He says, "*But with God all things are possible*" (NIV). *With God.* With God, anything can be achieved, even a change in attitude, even forgiveness.

Most times when we undergo any kind of hurt, the fight or flight instinct kicks in. When this happens, different things can occur. We may want to stay in the situation to inflict pain on the other party. Another option can be defensive. We may want to stand our ground and defend ourselves. The other alternative may be the desire to get away and protect ourselves.

I think that our responses will be different depending on the situation. For many years, I reasoned that if I never forgave past hurts, then I wouldn't let my guard down, and then no one could hurt me again. Nothing could be further from the truth; building those walls causes so much heartache and hurt. Distance between the builder and everyone around grows. All those walls serve to do is isolate us further and further from any love and fellowship that people are willing to share.

I had created a bubble world around me, but I didn't stop there. Outside of the bubble, I put up walls of stone, brick, concrete, and a six-inch layer of steel! It's not easy to break through those defences. That kind of wall serves to keep people out. They are supposed to create a safe haven, but do they? No. They create a prison, a place where the body and soul begin to dry out and shrivel up. The heart becomes hardened. Trust is far away.

Let me tell you one gigantic problem with those walls. The moment *will* come when you realize that you are all alone. When that happens, it's not pretty. Those walls, that took so much time and care to build, don't move easily. They take time to tear down. They didn't go up overnight and they won't come down overnight.

However, the truth to focus on is this. With God's help, the walls will come down. As soon as you make the decision to trust God, the walls will begin to crumble. He can bring them down completely and free you from the prison you built for yourself. He's done it for me and He can do it for you.

Forgiveness is one of those things that does not come naturally to everyone. Some of us have to work at it. It takes time to learn forgiveness. If you have lived (or continue to live) with unforgiveness and holding grudges, you can make a conscious decision to pray and ask for the help you need to train yourself differently. Living with all that anger, hate, and distrust does not punish the one who hurt you. It only punishes the one holding the grudge.

Jesus was very specific with His words about forgiveness. My favourite version comes from the Amplified Bible. "*For if you forgive people their trespasses [their reckless and willful sins, leaving them, letting them go, and giving up resentment], your heavenly Father will also forgive you. But if you do not forgive others their trespasses, [their reckless and willful sins, leaving them, letting them go, and giving up resentment], neither will your Father forgive you your trespasses*" (Matthew 6:14-15, AMP).

Now, really stop and take some time to think about that. Reread that Scripture again. Soak it up. Study the truth in Jesus' words. I recommend you pull out your own Bible. Check other versions. They all say the same basic thing. We *must* learn to forgive. Let's back up a bit and look at verse twelve: "*And forgive us our debts, as we also have forgiven (left, remitted, and let go of the debts, and have given up resentment against) our debtors*" (Matthew 6:12, AMP).

Do you really want God to forgive you like you forgive those who have hurt you? If your answer is no, I think you need to search your heart and see why. Consider this: "*For with what judgment you judge, you will be judged; and with the measure you use, it will be measured back to you*" (Matthew 7:2). Mighty sharp words. Words found in Scripture are timeless and mean the same thing to us as they did to the readers when the Bible was written.

When I finally saw Matthew 16:14-15 with loving eyes, eyes that my Saviour gave me to see with, I finally realized that I cannot hold grudges. It is now clear that I cannot keep feelings of unforgiveness and resentment toward anyone. Not for any reason, not for any length of time. That sounds severe, doesn't it? However, if I do hold those negative feelings toward others, how can I expect God to forgive me? His words are clear on the matter. Jesus died on the cross to forgive our sins. Who are we to decide who deserves forgiveness and who doesn't? Nobody, that's who. We are forgiven, and therefore we need to pass it on to others.

Forgiveness is a commandment from God. Do not try to go it alone. Through the power of the Holy Spirit, we are able to forgive. If we try to do it without prayer and the power of God, we may succeed for a time, but our success will be short lived. Ephesians 4:32, explains how we need to forgive: "*And be kind to one another, tender-hearted, forgiving one another, even as God in Christ forgave you.*" When Jesus was on the cross, He asked God to forgive His executioners (Luke 23:34). He died the most degrading, shameful death possible, yet He still asked forgiveness for those who did it to Him. When we say, "I cannot forgive," don't we mean "I don't want to forgive"?

If you are struggling with the concept of forgiveness, know that Jesus understands. He can heal your wounded soul and He wants to. Open up the innermost part of your soul to Him, allowing Him to spread the healing balm that you need to cleanse your soul now and forevermore. He is waiting for you.

Epilogue

God's promises to us are true, something we can count on. In a world where horrible things happen each and every day, it is comforting to know that we have a Saviour who loves us so much. In studying these promises, God has revealed more and more to me. I am constantly amazed by Him and His love for each of us. I pray that you will get hungry for His promises. Study the Scriptures prayerfully and allow the truth to take root in your heart and soul.

This is by no means a complete list of His promises, but only a beginning. As I searched for truth, at the beginning of my walk with Him, I was looking for truths I could apply to my own life. He has shown me how to seek out and apply Scripture in an incredible way. I pray that Jesus will come and fill your heart with the truth that produces an awesome change in your life. I know He has made a wonderful difference in mine.

May you always, "*Let your light so shine before men, that they may see your good works and glorify your Father in heaven*" (Matthew 5:16).

Blessings,
NATALIE

A Prayer for Salvation

Father in Heaven,

I come before You today knowing that I am a sinner. I am not worthy of Your love or forgiveness. I realize that what I do deserve is death. I believe that You sent Your one and only Son, Jesus Christ, to this earth, to live and then die for my sins. I believe with my whole heart that You raised Him on the third day and that He is alive today. Please forgive me, Lord, for all the wrong things in my life. I pray, asking for your forgiveness. By faith, I receive Your gift of salvation so I may be with You for all eternity. I give You my life as an offering. Thank You for being Lord of my life. In Jesus' name, Amen.

About the Author

Natalie is a speaker, author, and Bible teacher. She has led book studies in her home and teaches weekly Bible classes at her home church, Havelock Wesleyan, in Havelock, Nova Scotia. Her teaching style has been described as genuine, sensitive, and Spirit-led. In 2006, Natalie became a CLASS Communicator through ClassServices Inc. She makes her home in the quaint village of Weymouth with her wonderful husband Rollie and their three beautiful daughters whom she home schools.